WORTHY OF LIFE AND LOVE

A Journey through Tragedy and Loss to Finding Strength in God's Love

Kavanaugh Dickson Williams

WORTHY OF LIFE AND LOVE. Copyright © 2020. Kavanaugh Dickson Williams.

All rights reserved. No portion of this book may be reproduced, stored in a retrieval system, or transmitted in any form or by any means – electronic, mechanical, photocopy, recording, scanning, or other – except for a brief quotation in critical reviews or articles, without the prior written permission of the publisher or author.

Published by:

DAYELight
PUBLISHERS

ISBN: 978-1-949343-67-0 (paperback)

Scriptures taken from the New Century Version®. Copyright © 2005 by Thomas Nelson. Used by permission. All rights reserved.

Scriptures taken from the Holy Bible, New International Version®, NIV®. Copyright © 1973, 1978, 1984, 2011 by Biblica, Inc.™ Used by permission of Zondervan. All rights reserved worldwide. www.zondervan.com The "NIV" and "New International Version" are trademarks registered in the United States Patent and Trademark Office by Biblica, Inc.™

Scripture quotations marked NLT are taken from the *Holy Bible*, New Living Translation, copyright © 1996, 2004, 2015 by Tyndale House Foundation. Used by permission of Tyndale House Publishers, Inc., Carol Stream, Illinois 60188. All rights reserved.

Scripture quotations from New Revised Standard Version Bible, copyright © 1989 National Council of the Churches of Christ in the

United States of America. Used by permission. All rights reserved worldwide.

Scriptures marked as "(GNT)" are taken from the Good News Translation - Second Edition © 1992 by American Bible Society. Used by permission.

Scripture quotations are from The ESV® Bible (The Holy Bible, English Standard Version®), copyright © 2001 by Crossway, a publishing ministry of Good News Publishers. Used by permission. All rights reserved.

For information on booking the author for signings, interviews, and other events, contact Kavanaugh Dickson Williams by emailing ladykavanwrites@gmail.com

Dedication

I dedicate this book to the Birch boys: Matthew, Isaiah and Christopher.

As I reflect on the impact my first husband, Christopher Birch, had on me, I am grateful. It is impossible to interact with such a light and not be changed by it. Our covenant of marriage ended with your passing but my vow before God is this: "I will teach the boys about who you are and the sacrifices you made for them. I will honour your memory always. How can I do less when I see you in them every day? I will grow them as we planned it: in the fear and admonition of the Lord. Your sacrifice will not be in vain." Thanks for helping God teach me that I am *Worthy of Life and Love*.

To you, my reader, my prayer is that as I unveil the secrets of my heart and the experiences of my life, you will see God's grace and love inscribed on every page. I pray that you will see Him and accept His unfathomable love for you because that revelation will change you forever.

Acknowledgement

I try to live with a profound sense of gratitude everyday. I realize that I could have, and should have, been dead and I therefore take nothing for granted.

God, I want to thank You for loving me because of who You are, not for who I was, am or will be. I am grateful for the gift of words and for the strength You gave me to share them with the world. I am nothing without You.

To my amazing husband, who continues to be a safe space for my heart, I love you beyond words. Thanks for supporting me as I write this story.

To my parents and brother, you undergirded me in the darkest moments of my life, thank you. My home team, i.e., my friends who are family, thanks for keeping me sane, grounded and loved. This story is also yours because I could not have written it without you.

Michelle Ross Williams, thank you for obeying your assignment in my life to be my mentor, friend and sister. I appreciate the time you took to write the endearing foreword.

Finally, to my church family, friends, social media supporters, well-wishers, brothers and sisters in Christ, thank you for the prayers, encouragement and support.

To my proofreaders, graphic designer; Staysean Daley, DayeLight Publishers and your team, thanks for helping to bring my vision to life. I am forever grateful.

May God return to you all a thousand-fold for all the support you give.

Table of Contents

Dedication v

Acknowledgement vii

Foreword 11

Introduction 15

Preface 17

Section 1
"Walk With Me"

Chapter One: The Breaking 21

Chapter Two: The Girl Who Was Touched Wrong 27

Chapter Three: Finding A Light 35

Chapter Four: A Love Like No Other 39

Chapter Five: A Love Worth Dying For 47

Chapter Six: I Ran 55

Chapter Seven: As A Man Thinks So Is He 65

Section 2
"A Letter For You"

A Letter To My Younger Self 75

A Letter To The Widow 81

A Letter To The Married Singles 85

A Letter To The Single Parent 88

A Letter To The Woman Seeking Love 93

A Letter To The Divorcee 97

A Letter To The Married Woman 103

Now That I Know 107

Section 3
"Affirmations"

Daily Affirmations 113

About The Author 119

Foreword

It is an honour and a privilege to write this foreword, as well as knowing Kavanaugh for a number of years. I met her when she and her now deceased first husband, Christopher, came to worship at our church. They were such a wonderful couple and exemplified God's guidance in the middle of their marriage. She was a young lady accomplished in academia and in the arts and on fire for God. She was very active in the church and her area of expertise and greatest love was with the youth. They loved and respected her, and felt they had a safe place in her to share their distresses and teenage challenges. She then became a mother and I watched as she lovingly cared for her two boys and the family. She was always dependable, reliable and always knew when to be quiet, as if she was processing what was taking place around her. She is a loyal friend and was always willing to help anyone who needed her help. She was all things to all people.

I was also there when the worst day of her life came. She suffered the greatest traumatic loss of her life, which left her in a tailspin. She still tried to be all things to all people. She held it together for the boys and herself, and she had great difficulties with her loving Father – Jesus. She struggled and had a battle with God and His form of love for her. Her grief was hard, and her loss was great, but in time she found His loving care and grace and was able to slowly start seeing the light at the end of the tunnel. Her healing process was evident through her first book—a devotional titled "Grief Stricken." In that book, she takes the bereaved through eight days of devotions to a final place of peace.

This book is her continued path through the healing process of her life, and I am very proud of her. I have watched her with her boys and how she cares for them and as a new wife and how she is charting a new course in her life.

Worthy of Life and Love is a raw, real, retrospective, revelatory, refreshing, and revealing book. It will have you engaged from start to finish as she takes readers through the ebbs and flows of her life as she discovered herself, and who she is in Christ Jesus. Kavanaugh has used this book as her own catharsis, and chronicles her journey through a life besieged by challenges, but reflects and showcases victories, tenacity, resilience, healing, forgiveness, and discovering a deeper relationship with God, who initially seemed not to have been there but was through it all. It is certain to touch the lives of those who read these pages.

Kavanaugh has made herself vulnerable, and readers will be provoked to come to their own understanding of who God is in their own lives and find a love that surpasses all human understanding. It is a must-read for those who have encountered great loss, sexual abuse, and running away from God. Using Scriptures and the characters therein, Kavanaugh is able to guide readers through grace, hope, repentance, the loving hands and patient heart of God.

She has poured her inner soul into this book and invites readers to journey with her as a widow, a single mother ensuring her young sons do not lose sight of their earthly father's influence, while guiding them into the heavenly Father's love and grace; a daughter, sister, friend and wife. This soul-searching and Scripture-based book will help readers recognize that all is not lost when heartbreak comes knocking, but that through the storms and gales of life, the winds will abate, the skies will again turn blue, and the sun will shine again, with the help and loving guidance of the Son of God.

Michelle A. Williams, LLB
Associate Counselling Psychologist
Minister, Mentor and Friend

Introduction

Since the passing of my first husband, I get asked in a dozen ways: "How did you make it? Why are you not crazy?" I have also heard how strong I am. My response is usually to say: "I don't know" or "Oh no, I'm not strong. It wasn't me; it was God." I cringed inside because the truth is, I do not know, nor do I understand how I survived. I just know that I did and *Who* helped me do it.

This book is a memoir of sorts. In these pages, I have shared some personal and difficult truths about my journey and how that led me to the conclusion that I am "Worthy of Life and Love." This book has three sections: Section one is titled "Walk With Me" and it chronicles what I remember to be crucial junctions in my life and the lessons God patiently taught, even before I was ready to fully accept them. Section two is titled "Letters For You" and it contains seven letters of encouragement, addressed to specific groups of people I particularly identify with and have a message for. They are not meant to be universal or all-encompassing. Finally, Section 3 is titled "Affirmations" and it contains twenty-one Scripture-based affirmations to help you water the soil of your heart and help you to live in the truth about how much God loves you.

I must warn you; this book is raw and personal. It is intended for women who have experienced sexual or emotional abuse and gives insight into how that may have affected your psyche, decision-making process, proclivities, and/or personality. The hope is to juxtapose such experiences with God's intention for your life. When we cling to the truth that we are loved beyond measure or reason, something shifts in the atmosphere of our hearts and we will never be the same. I imagine this could have been the revelation alive in Horatio G. Spafford's heart when he penned the song "It Is Well With My Soul" in the midst of a heart-wrenching tragedy. This song has become mine to sing as well. It is my prayer that after reading this book, it will be yours to sing too.

Preface

The sun rested sweetly over the garden of the Pegasus Hotel in New Kingston on a Monday morning in the summer of 2007. Bright orange and yellow petals flowered the aisle where brooms were vibrantly decorated to form a pathway to the white gazebo. Guests were beautifully dressed as they lifted brightly colored Chinese umbrellas to provide shade. The bride was a few minutes late and flustered because her makeup artist did not show up and someone else had to fill in. Her heart was anxious, not from the thoughts relating to the arrangements of the day, but rather her worthiness for the role she was about to play.

She never felt deserving of him; *he was too good and pure of a soul to handle her brokenness,* she thought. She loved him more than she could express, and he was absolutely clear that he would stop at nothing to prove to her that not all men intended to bring her pain. So, she shoved her anxiety aside, locked arms with her father and walked composed but slowly down the aisle.

When he read his vow, there was silence for a few seconds and there were quiet sobs from the audience. She was a mess with tears and his words washed her anxiety away. This was a new start. Fairy tales were real, and this was her Knight looking dapper in a tux. To bring you in on the profundity of that moment, here is an excerpt of the said vow:

"My Father declares that greater love hath no man than this: that a man lay down his life for his friends. Thus, it is in accordance with His Word and with my heart: my friend, my companion, my empress, my wife, that I lay down my life before you today. It is upon this sacrifice that I pledge these things to you. I vow to be your companion, a constant source of support, comfort, strength, reproof, and rebuke. I vow to be your priest, to stand in the gap for you, to be your teacher, to be the bearer of the Word, the Word that pierces even to the dividing asunder of your soul and spirit."

I was the bride that morning in July. I was filled with the hope that nothing in my past could taint this miracle my heavenly Father had graciously given. Like every marriage, we had our share of trials, especially within the first two years. We separated for six months to reset but when we came back together, it was a whole new us with one vision. He honored every word of his vow and until the moment he was stolen from us, I lived with the notion that no matter how the enemy of our souls would huff and puff, he could never blow our house down again, until he did.

SECTION 1

"WALK WITH ME"

Chapter One

The Breaking

Praise the Lord; praise God our Saviour! For each day he carries us in His arms. (Psalm 68:19 – NLT).

It was the kind of scene you see in movies: yellow tape, police sirens, and crowds of curious onlookers. Perhaps for the sake of my sanity, my brain has shut down my memory of it. But my friends tell me how I laid on the ground screaming, bawling, praying, and how I seemed, after a while, to just be in a daze. A few hours before this scene, thieves invaded our home and stole various items and my first husband's life. My world shattered; every plan, every dream, in moments, they all disappeared like drops of water on desert sand.

It was more than any of us could fathom. A million questions plagued our minds and rocked our souls. How could the saintliest of beings we know die -- like *that*? He did nothing to deserve it. We are Christians. Did we do something wrong? Had we failed to pray? Had God somehow been asleep that night? Why did He allow this? How *could* He allow it? Where was the protection we were promised?

Your story may not be as dramatic as mine or maybe it is far more. But the questions are familiar to everyone who has undergone a really difficult time in their lives. Where is God? I will not attempt to answer that question theologically, this is not what this is about. But, experientially, when I look back a few years later, I imagine He was right there being touched by my brokenness. I am convinced that Jesus wept that day and as inconceivable as it was for me during that season, He held me that day and in the weeks and months to follow.

I am jumping ahead again so let us get back to the story.

Superhuman strength is accessible in the midst of a community that rallies around you in the midst of your pain. They carry you, hold you, and help you take the steps you need to in order to make it to the next thing. My family, my friends, his friends and church community were awesome. They were a gift for which I am forever grateful. In the weeks leading up to the funeral, I did not have much time between planning, house hunting and being distracted by the many faces that would come and go offering support. I embraced my faith like it was all I had because it felt like it was all I had left.

As life would have it, there is life after someone has passed. Everyone, without meaning to, must get on with their own lives and walk their own paths. You, the bereaved, must get on with the business of life. It was there in the silence that my faith waned thin. It was in the silence that the questions came at me like gale-force winds and my "doctoral in churchiology" did not hold up to the hurricane besetting my mind. Where was God? Where were the angels assigned to my protective detail?

I read through many of the Scriptures that promised protection and my heart broke even more. They felt like a lie and if one thing was a lie, then all of it was a lie. I lost it. I lost my faith and my will to live. I did not eat without being forced to and I certainly could not sleep without that little pill. I could not look at the boys without a thousand daggers attacking my heart because I could see him still in their eyes and in their mannerisms.

More than these questions, guilt came creeping to the surface and haunted me like a horrid horror movie. Guilt? For what? Well, I used to tell my students and mentees that I was not born saved and even after I found Christ, I was "the try it at least once" kind of person. I had a "Jesus come save me AGAIN" complex. Some of you might know it. I mess up, He chases me, I feel guilty but amazed at His love and His choosing to forgive me one more time and then I would work really hard to "prove to Him" that I was worthy of His salvation. But then it takes so much energy, so I try something else and --- you get the point!

So, at that point the enemy is whispering quite convincingly that it was something I did that opened the door. I did not pray enough. I was not spiritual enough. I was not worthy of this man so God took him early from me. Or maybe I had stepped into some spiritual battle unprepared and that was the backlash. The thoughts and emotions reverberated through my soul like a loud gong. It was all I could hear. So, I chose to believe the lie.

I called this winter season of my life the "Great Sadness," which is an apt title I took from W.P Young's "The Shack" (awesome book, by the way, I highly recommend it but I digress). The sadness hovered like a cloud I could not evade. In public, I smiled and wore a brave face like a mask. At home, I would take it off and crumble into a pile of uncontrollable sorrow. I would gather all my strength to ensure that the boys had as normal a life as possible. I made sure they could play, have the things they liked to eat and were kept busy with activities. I thought maybe if they were busy enough, they would not notice the gaping hole in their lives. It was my strategy too: Busy Bee Kavanaugh.

After a while, feigned strength fails. My therapist, Dr. C. Johnson, picked up on it and designed a getaway weekend to jumpstart my endorphins (happy hormones). I had to do it alone. I had to embrace my new reality. I was not a "we" anymore, I was a "me." It was a jolting reality shock but a well-needed one. I had to accept that my "life plan" had changed.

I am going to let you in on a secret. I am a planner, so much so that I knew I needed to finish university at age twenty-one. I knew I had to find my husband there so we could get married at twenty-five. I knew I needed my Masters degree before thirty. I knew I wanted two children and we would start after about three years of marriage. But life events have a way of blindsiding you, knocking the wind out of you, and changing your trajectory. I learned that painfully well. How you come out on the other side depends on the foundational concepts you have buried inside.

So, here is the message, in case you do not get to the end of the book, although I hope you will. Regardless of your past or present circumstances, whether you chose it or it happened to you, you are worthy of LIFE and LOVE. I put those in capital letters because they are names: names God called Himself and all puns are intended. He thought you lovingly into existence before you were a seed in your mother's womb (See Psalms 139:13). He thought you were worth dying for (See Romans 5:10) and He thought you were worthy of the gift of life, and not just in the eternal ever after but here and now. Regardless of what you have done or failed to do; He still thinks so. He came that you may have life and have it more abundantly (See John 10:10).

Chapter Two

The Girl Who Was Touched Wrong

The Lord is near to the brokenhearted and saves the crushed in spirit. (Psalm 34:18 – ESV).

In Jamaica in 2016, they reported more than a thousand cases of sexual abuse in children. The US Department of Health and Human Services published a report in February 2018 called "Child Maltreatment 2016." It reported that 60,000 children were abused, of which 90% knew their perpetrators. The statistics are mind-blowing, especially considering that because of the nature of the crime, most cases go unreported. My cases were not reported. I could write a blurb here of what psychologists say about the impact of these things, but it would be superficial. So, let us talk about me. Obviously then, the impact is not a universal principle but I am sure I cannot be the only one impacted this way.

My first sexual encounter was with the neighbour, an older girl who went to the same primary school as I did. I suppose she was in her experimental "trying-to-discover-her-body" phase. Nothing major, it seemed at the time, but a little fondling. So, I played along. Something innately felt odd but since I could not pinpoint what that was, I assumed it was innocent and normal. Wrong! It was a seed. At six years old, maybe seven, I became aware that my body was sexual. More importantly, I realized its use, in that way, was a secret to be kept from my parents.

Then, there was playing "family" with older cousins and uncles. Being the only female in the crew, I was always mommy and whoever daddy was, he had the privilege of fondling mommy. That is what parents do when children are asleep, right? Again, I thought this was normal and, of course, something you never tell your parents. My mom always asked though. She would warn, she would remind: "Kavan, if anyone touches you in a way that does not feel right, let me know." But it was too late, I had already learned that these were "normal secret games" that adults did not need to know about.

Fast forward to my teen years. My dad had migrated, so it was just Mom and three children. My brothers and I shared a room, though not a bed. An adult cousin came to visit with us for a short while. One night, he came in drunk or intoxicated from marijuana and he tried to rape me. I was confused. This was not a game I willingly participated in and he was not listening to me saying no. Fortunately, he was too "out of it" to be focused on being successful in his efforts. But what he did was enough to ejaculate on my clothes, leaving me feeling violated and nasty. I waited until morning and I told my mother. What comes next is very important.

She checked me thoroughly, confirmed a hundred times that he did not penetrate, got me cleaned up and told me to stay inside. My cousin was outside with my brothers either oblivious to what he had done or was playing it cool. I watched as my mother spent a long time sharpening her machete and staring intensely at my cousin. When she launched at him, the gleam of the sun from the machete caught his eye and he was able to run before she caught him. She threw his things outside and he was forever banned from the house.

My mom was angry. She was being protective; she had my back. But what my brain began to calculate was on another level. What if she had hurt him? I would have lost my mother to prison and we would end up in foster care or some other reality that was not acceptable to me. I vowed then that whatever happened to me in the future, I would not tell my mother because I could not risk losing her. Her attempt to protect me pushed me further into secrecy.

It was as if I wore an invisible sign after that: "available for abuse." The guys seemed to see it. I did not know why. The incidents after that escalated. There was the boyfriend who felt it necessary to lock me in a room until I gave in. My first encounter with the full act of sex, the act God designed to show love between two married, committed people, was coerced. There was a family friend who was supposed to take me home but stopped at his house and lured me by telling me people were home, the lights were on. It was a quick stop and coming inside would be safer than staying in the car by myself. All lies.

The first seed planted told me it was okay for an adult or older child to fondle me as long as it was a game. This diminished for me the sense of value I should have for my own body. As I got older, it meant saying no took a lot more effort than it should. If someone made me slightly uncomfortable, I would tolerate it. Often, it was not until things were really uncomfortable or I was in real danger that I mustered the energy to run. The other two main incidents made me think I was unworthy of the wait and the choice for a sexual partner; that my body was for exploit and no one would love me beyond what they could see physically; that my heart, mind and soul were unworthy of knowing.

The Bible is not silent on this matter. When Dinah, the daughter of Jacob and Leah, was raped by a prince called Shechem, Genesis 34:7b says: "They were shocked and furious that their sister had been raped. Shechem had done a **disgraceful thing** against Jacob's family, something that should never be done" (NLT – emphasis mine). So disgraceful was this act that her brothers killed Shechem and all the men in his city.

When men from the Tribe of Benjamin gang-raped a man's unnamed concubine and left her for dead in Judges 19–21, civil war broke out. No, I am not saying we should go around and murder rapists, but I am saying that sins of this nature were so offensive that justice was immediate and swift in Biblical times.

Today, I hear more shame for victims of sexual abuse than I hear of justice. Even as I write, I am scared of what will be said. "You were raped? Did you cause this? Are you sure you did not give him the go-ahead? I mean, you did know he was home alone and that "let's watch TV upstairs" was a code that he wanted to do more." NO, I DID NOT KNOW. I DID NOT ASK FOR THIS. Then, why did I feel broken, unusable, and unworthy of anything good? Why did I feel undeserving of God's best? Because this is the ultimate lie of sexual abuse. It is a violation of your body and soul. The act that was meant to communicate love was instead used to spew hate. It causes a weird dyslexion of the soul that impacts your ability to identify, much less receive and appreciate love. It is hard to interpret a good touch from a bad one, when the memory of the bad one becomes the glasses through which you view life. In his piece titled "Just God", Poet Ezekiel Azonwu put it this way: "...molestation says I hate you while using an act that was designed to say I love you. No wonder her heart had grown dyslexic, what a wretched collage of mixed messages."

Sexual abuse is not new but the effects on a person's psyche are far-reaching and destiny-impacting. For me, sex and sexuality became a twisted thing. Secrecy was comforting. I was fine with having a different persona to the different people in my life. I was one thing to my friends, and another thing to the adults in my life.

When I became a Christian, the struggle deepened. My secret struggles had to remain secret because who would love and accept me with flaws and all, when the image required for my new life was perfection? In this new life, the virgins were lauded and accepted, and the non-virgins were shown the back seat like lepers who had to shout "unclean" as though their disease was all there was to them. As a church, we seem to push the lost and broken away, as if we were not designed to be a hospital for broken souls.

For the parents reading this: do not get scared - get vigilant. A whopping 90% of sexual abuse cases in children happen with people they know. Start early. I was explaining private parts to my children and who is allowed to touch them, before they could talk. I gave them the protocol: "Tell mommy if someone touched you and you did not like it." I did not tolerate people entering their personal space without their say so and if they complained, I honoured it by not being dismissive.

Most importantly though, I try not to overreact when they share information with me (for any topic) so they could always feel comfortable telling me what is on their heart. For example, my older son, Matt, shared with me some struggles he was having while grieving his father. My heart must have been shattering in a million pieces; I could hear it breaking. I mustered all the strength of Christ in me and addressed his concerns empathetically and comfortingly. When I left his room, I went into mine, closed the door and wept. My processing and emotion would be too much for him to process and I could not risk him concluding that when he tells mommy something, she gets too sad or angry, so he would not share anything else.

As I share this bit of my history, I reflect on how much time and energy I spent battling the insecurities, pain, assault on my psyche that these incidents scattered throughout my childhood caused. I wish this older self was able to whisper in my teen ear: "It's not your fault. You are beautiful on the inside too. You are worthy of the best. Do not downplay your talents and abilities because you fear you will give your all and still be thought of as not good enough." I would warn my younger self not to dim my light in fear of being truly seen. I would quote Psalm 139 over and over so it would not just be theory but reality. What I am grateful for is that God never gives up and He chases us relentlessly until, finally, His truth sets us free.

Chapter Three

Finding A Light

I am the light of the world. Whoever follows me will not walk in darkness, but will have the light of life. (John 8:12b – ESV).

When I was a little girl, I loved to run barefooted outside. Wearing shoes to play outside was not a thing. I remember one day a piece of broken glass sliced the space between my big toe and the next. My parents dressed the wound, being careful to remove any pieces of glass they found. Soon enough the toe appeared to be healing and all was right with my world again. It may have been about a year later that the toe started to hurt in the same spot. It was not an ignorable pain but sharp pains. The area itched and I could not figure it out. Eventually, the wound opened up and became a sore. It was bizarre. We soon discovered that a shard of glass was still lodged in my foot. After a year of pretending everything was okay, my body started to reject this foreign object, pushing it to the surface.

Soul wounds have a similar modus operandi. We often live with shards of broken glass just beneath the surface of our psyche, unaware of how deeply they affect us. One day though, your soul will begin to reject this hidden pain and push it to the surface. It manifests in our attitudes, biases, and proclivities towards sin. If we are not careful, this sore will poison our relationships and sabotage our purpose.

As I continued to pursue life with Christ, I was embroiled in an internal battle between the me I wanted to be and the pain that lay brewing under the surface. I had assumed a pious, innocent, joyful, outward appearance but my heart was burdened with self-doubt, self-hate, and all kinds of insecurities. The duplicity manifested in the ways I rejected some healthy relationships and toyed with others that were blatantly, undeniably relationships and escapades I had no business being involved in.

I believe all behaviour patterns persist because it provides some internal reward and satisfaction. For me, dark, secret-type relationships were my soul's way of hanging on to a familiar pain. Each time I connected to it, it made it real in a sense. It was almost as if I needed to justify the reason for walking around with this dull ache all the time. It gave me a reason to cry out to God to save me again. New wounds and reasons to be rescued meant I could keep dealing with symptoms and not the root cause.

Somewhere around the second year of university, my soul wound began to itch. It became a little more difficult to hide but I tried anyway. It was in that same year I met Christopher, who would become my husband five years later. That thought was inconceivable then of course. Chris was in his "Paul Phase." He was convinced he would never get married and that he wanted to be like Paul: sold out to the Gospel and nothing else.

He was peculiar to me. Unlike the men that typically drew close to me, he seemed totally disinterested in me physically yet absolutely committed to my growth spiritually, emotionally, and academically. It was weird. He was chivalrous and a total gentleman. It was impossible for me to construe his behaviour as an indication of interest because he was that way to every woman he met. His light shone in such a way that it called into question my internal theory that all men had a secret agenda. We became friends: the kind of friends that hung out, helped each other, spoke deeply about their issues, prayed yet remained platonic.

I recall one night, those glass shards pushing to the surface of my soul caused a panic attack so exhausting that I thought of ending my life. I lived on campus and, fortunately, my friends were there to rescue. I cannot recall now how Chris found out, whether I told him, or he heard from a friend. He became pensive and solemn. Timidly I asked what he was thinking. I expected judgement or a sermon on how disappointed he was that I would conceive of such an idea. Instead, when he eventually spoke, he said, "I am trying to imagine what I would have done if I lost you."

Our relationship took on a different tone. His proposal at the time was for us to work together to accomplish God's purpose for each other's lives. So it was that he continued to be one of God's ways of shining His light on my heart. He constantly reminded me who I belonged to and washed my heart with God's Word. But do you know that light can feel offensive for those comfortable in the dark? I didn't hate the light and I was genuine in my Christian faith, but I had broken places I had not surrendered to His healing. Therefore, I could not grasp the fullness of the light, I could not see it. Luke 11:34 says "Your eye is like a lamp that provides light for your body. When your eye is healthy, your whole body is filled with light. But when it is unhealthy, your body is filled with darkness" (NLT). There are two possible responses when the light of God's Word hits you: you can choose to look at what it reveals and cooperate with the Holy Spirit to transform or you can become insular and try to hide the exposed area in shame.

For me, pain was comfortable – it was what I knew. In Psalm 139: 11, David declared a thought familiar to me. He said: "I could ask the darkness to hide me and the light around me to become night" (NLT). Instead of embracing those lessons, I believed the lies that I was undeserving of all the affection and love God lavished. My eyes were closed to the truth. I am grateful that David's thought did not end there. He reminds us that there is a but: "Even in darkness I cannot hide from you. To you the night shines as bright as day. Darkness and light are the same to you" (Psalm 139: 12 - NLT). God renews His mercy towards us every day. He has always been more interested in our heart position than in our actions, so He continues to pursue us in Love. Knowing our whys, He patiently waits to win every area of our hearts to Him.

Chapter Four

A Love Like No Other

...love covers all offenses. (Proverbs 10:12b – ESV)

There is a beautiful allegory in Scripture that describes a marriage filled with love, drama, pain, and redemption. If we were to produce a movie or a series based on this story, it would have us on the edge of our seats. However, the most awesome thing about this story is that it had nothing to do with the actual husband and wife and everything to do with Christ and His Church, more specifically, more personally, Jesus and the depth of His inexplicable love for me. I want to spend some time on it here because when you truly get this story on a heart level, it will change your life. It did for me.

We do not know Gomer's backstory, but we know that God told Hosea to marry a prostitute as an example of his relationship with His people. God was explicit. He said: "Go and marry a prostitute, so that some of her children will be conceived in prostitution. This will illustrate how Israel has acted like a prostitute by turning against the Lord and worshipping other gods" (Hosea 1:2b – NLT). This was not a fairy-tale like the 1990's classic "Pretty Woman," where the prostitute met a wonderful guy, he changed her life, and she never went back to that lifestyle again. Hosea went into the relationship fully aware that it was going to be painful: Gomer was going to cheat and his job was to love her still.

Let us pause for a moment: do we realize that God, being omniscient, that is, all-knowing, is fully aware of every heartbreak we will cause Him and yet He relentlessly chases us without concern for His own pain? How many of us would run full force towards someone, if we knew there was even a slight chance they would reject us? For the most part, people do not enter marriage covenants lightly. Neither does God. He created humans with free will. Our worshipping Him in truth must be a choice. It is the risk He takes to win true affection; our affection.

The language and tone of the writing in Hosea is potent and fervent and a little uncomfortable. Written from God's perspective, God sounds like a lover who is really angry because His bride is not giving Him the attention He craves. It is the kind of monologue you expect from a deeply wounded soul. Why is God so worked up? Why does He even use the metaphor He did? Why is He comparing Israel to a married prostitute? Since He is God, He does have the world and everyone in it at His disposal so why be so ruffled by infidelity? The answer is simple yet absolutely profound: LOVE.

1 John 4:8 declares that God is love. Love is not what God does or gives; it is who He is. Love is His very character and nature, inseparable from His personality and actions. Have you ever read the amplified version of 1 Corinthians 13? Read

it and replace the word Love with God and we get a beautiful picture of God's passion for us:

> Love *(God)* endures long and is patient and kind; love *(God)* never is envious nor boils over with jealousy, is not boastful or vainglorious, does not display itself *(Himself)* haughtily. It *(He)* is not conceited (arrogant and inflated with pride); it *(He)* is not rude (unmannerly) and does not act unbecomingly. Love *(God)* does not insist on its *(His)* own rights or its *(His)* own way, for it *(He)* is not self-seeking; it *(He)* is not touchy or fretful or resentful; it *(He)* takes no account of the evil done to it *(Him)* [*(He)* it pays no attention to a suffered wrong]. It *(He)* does not rejoice at injustice and unrighteousness, but rejoices when right and truth prevail. Love *(God)* bears up under anything and everything that comes, is ever ready to believe the best of every person, its (*His*) hopes are fadeless under all circumstances, and it *(He)* endures everything [without weakening]. Love (*God*) never fails [never fades out or becomes obsolete or comes to an end]. (1 Corinthians 13:4-8 – AMP – emphasis mine).

Getting back to the story of Hosea and Gomer, we now have a deeper glimpse of why, in spite of her infidelity, God's instruction to Hosea is to pursue her. He puts obstacles in her way to make it difficult for her to seek her lovers but it is her choice anyway. One day, Gomer does not return from her escapades. She decides it is better to leave her position as wife, as co-manager of a household, to live as a prostitute full time. She is sold into slavery and from the auction blocks her husband purchases her; he buys her back. He had all the right to treat her as a slave in his household because that is what she had become. He could have used his position as the master to teach her a lesson for her betrayal and the shame she brought on him as a man of God and the embarrassment her children undoubtedly faced in their daily lives. Instead, he did not hold her humongous sin against her. He invites her home and reinstated her position first as betrothed or his fiancé for a period of cleansing and then restored as wife.

God is persistent and consistent. His Love is relentless and ridiculous to human consciousness. It makes no sense, yet it is tangible and very real. We are all spiritual Gomers. We chase lesser loves and insist on holding on to the familiar, rather than embracing the new covenant of Love that has been given to us. We sit in a palace filled with all we need and stare out the window at what we had or want. We see God as one who restricts, rather than frees. We perceive His protection as a prison and mope like the children of Israel about the wonders of Egypt, the place that held us in captivity. Why? We have failed to embrace Him as the Lover of our souls. He does not just want to keep us from a hell not intended or designed for us, He longs to meet with us in the cool of the day to fellowship with the children He created.

Parenting and marriage have expanded my concept of love immensely. I love my boys. For the most part, they are great children, but they often get on my very last nerve. I repeat the same instructions day in and day out, yet it is treated like new information each time. Regardless of how frustrated I get; my love is a constant unending stream. I love them so deeply that I would sacrifice my life for theirs without thinking. They fill me with joy as they are clumsy and excited about every new discovery.

As a wife, my most important earthly relationship is with my husband. We sacrifice for each other, prioritise each other, and work on building deep intimacy. That relationship is guarded and protected from any third-party influence. We expect kids to grow up and move away, friends to leave but the expectation of a spouse is that death, not debt, is the only thing that should separate us. It is the reason why divorce is so painful and difficult. It was not meant to be that way.

When God calls us His bride, it presents us with an imagery of deep intimacy. It is a covenant between two people who choose every day to prioritise each other and put the needs of their spouse above their own. This synchronisation creates unity. It spoiled my theology when I realized that the God of all that is, is interested in being one with me. He chooses to store His limitless treasure in earthen, that is, frail vessels like me. Jesus said, "I and the Father are one" (John 10:30 - NIV). He lived out of that synchronisation every day. It was this consciousness of His Father's presence and intimacy that made His life effective. Now that I have grasped, to some extent, God's desire to express His love to me, in me, and through me to a broken world, I can understand when God uses a word such as "prostitute" to describe this bride. It literally breaks His heart when we give our affection to lesser gods and things that have no ability to satisfy our deepest hunger.

I remember when I happened upon this story many years ago. I was so impacted that I scripted a play about it for the Youth Department to present as a modern-day retake. I felt, in many ways, like a Gomer. I felt I was not good enough for my husband, and I lived in fear that he would discover it one day and walk away. I felt that although the other things I chased for attention were lesser loves, they felt more in line with what I thought of me: less is what I deserved. It was my subconscious way of preparing a plan B for when the "more" left. If it did, I could fall back on the less I should have had in the first place.

I think back now, and I want to weep for my warped thinking. How could I get stuck at the "go marry a prostitute" without meditating on the breadth of the story? I allowed my insecurity to establish the thought that God only saw me as a prostitute. I operated then out of fear. This fear kept me in a loop that would subconsciously taunt: "Work hard to become worthy of your relationship with God" and "Do not invest too much because it will not last." As I said in the previous chapter, light can be offensive if you hold to darkness or pain as a comfort blanket.

I encourage you to examine the evidence and embrace this infallible truth. You are loved by Love Himself. Say it: "God loves me." He loves you regardless of what you have done or failed to do. It is a love that requires nothing in return for it to exist. When we grab hold of it, we become so enamored that as we live out of God's love, everything else changes with significantly less effort than working to check off a list of dos and do nots.

CHAPTER FIVE

A Love Worth Dying For

"I am the good shepherd. The good shepherd gives his life for the sheep." (John 10:11 – NCV).

As I write this, we are in the season of Lent. It is the time of year we pause to deeply reflect on Christ's sacrifice for us. In the Book of Luke 7:47, Jesus speaks about the one who having been forgiven much loves much. I suppose the statement rings true for me because of my perspective on the much that I have been forgiven. As a Christian, the crux of my belief system is that Christ took the penalty, weight and consequence of my sins and died in my place. He died so that I could live. It is not a truth I take lightly. Recently, a colleague asked why a good person like Jesus had to die so gruesomely. Why did He have to die at all? Was there no other way? He kept repeating, "This makes no sense." I explained the concept that we were born sinful and that the requirement for the cleansing of sin required sacrifice: not just any sacrifice, but a pure one. So, God, in the magnitude of His love, sent His only Son to be that sacrifice for us. This is the Gospel. This is the centre of it all.

After the conversation, I left the room, but my thoughts began to reflect on Christopher. It was the kind of conversation that triggered a series of thoughts that getting distracted by the activities of the day did not appease. He died an unfitting death in his attempt to protect those he loved. My heart screamed: "It's just not fair!" It breaks my heart still. Until now, I have not spoken publicly about what happened that night. As you can imagine, recollecting it is deeply painful and invites king-wave type sorrow to wash the shores of my heart.

It was the first weekend in December and our close friend, Peta-Gaye, mother of our first godchild, was visiting from overseas. We packed up the boys and moved up our customary Boxing Day trip to Discovery Bay by a few weeks. We went to the beach. We laughed and reminisced about how beautiful change was. You see, we had been visiting that same spot every year for almost a decade. It was our tradition. Over time the routine grew to involve our children and the focus shifted from us being carefree on the beach, to us blowing up huge water toys so our children could play. In my mind's eye, that scene replayed like the perfect setup scene in a movie, where everything was perfect before something terrible happened.

We went home on Sunday so Chris could deliver a message to the men at church on the topic "Marriage and Fatherhood". I then spent the afternoon moderating games for a dear friend's baby shower. We got home late. I needed to study for an examination so I chose to sleep on the couch so I could bring myself to wake up to study and not disturb Chris. My mother, a close friend, and the two boys were also home.

I was stirred out of sleep perhaps by a draft of cold air hitting my face or an eerie feeling someone was in the room. When I opened my eyes, the front door, which I had closed before bed, was wide open. My eyes then shifted to a masked figure sneaking towards the table that had all the laptops and gadgets on it. In panic, I screamed. The armed man pointed the gun at me and told me to be quiet. The gun was still in my face when Chris ran out of the room having heard my screams. A struggle between the men ensued and shots were fired. The smell of gunpowder filled the room. Chris fell to the ground. Beyond the fear, beyond the panic, I kept praying for two things; keep him alive so we can get him to the hospital, and that no one else would be hurt. They locked us in the room to the rear of the house, while they rummaged for cash and valuables. When the gunman left, we struggled to get Chris into the car because, let's face it, waiting for an ambulance or the police in Jamaica would be pointless. He was pronounced dead at the hospital. My mind retreated to another place.

I cannot say I remember what I said or what I did when I had to leave Chris at the hospital. I returned home defeated and lost. My friend recalled that I was hysterical and arguing with God as my mind grappled with the events of the morning. I then became incoherent when I spoke, but mostly quiet. For the boys, my aim was to shield them from the trauma of the event. I told them Dad had gone to heaven so he would not be coming home. I did not tell them how.

In my devotional "Grief Stricken" I shared an excerpt from my journal on how I felt towards God during a high point of grief. Humanly speaking, our sense of justice cannot fathom the death of someone undeserving for the crimes of another. As the adage goes, "You commit the crime, you do the time." Doing someone else's time or paying for someone else's crime does not sit well with most people. I was advised that Christopher's unnamed killer was killed by police, while he attempted to do the same to another family. I must admit that I rejoiced for all of two minutes. What followed was the blaring gut-wrenching realisation that his death changed nothing. Chris was still gone, and my family was still broken. For this nameless masked ruiner of lives, there would be no trial, no demands for explanation, and no justice for us in this lifetime.

It makes absolutely no sense that God would come in the flesh to die a criminal's death to save humanity. We are decrepit and undeserving, from the murderer to the manipulator, and all sinners in between. Eternal death should be our reward. Yet Paul explains in Romans 5:7-8: "Very rarely will anyone die for a righteous person, though for a good person someone might possibly dare to die. But God demonstrates His own love for us in this: While we were still sinners, Christ died for us" (NIV). While we were still sinners; still not cognizant of our state; still not aware of His love nor able to acknowledge our need to be saved; before we could process the notion of it, Christ Jesus died. Christ died with the hope that we would come to accept Him. I think of how bravely and instinctively Christopher faced our attacker, with no thought of his own life. He knew we needed a hero that night and he volunteered to be him. This is Love.

If I were to do a poll, most of us have scales on which we rank good versus bad. We often think of ourselves as good people and we rank bad by how our actions impact others. Yet, Scripture holds no such distinction. Even the best among us are innately flawed and need to work on some aspect of ourselves. Romans 3:23 says: "For all have sinned and fall short of the glory of God" (NKJV). On the other end of the spectrum, there are some of us with self-esteem so shattered that "worthless", "no good" and "invaluable" are the internal descriptors for ourselves. I believe we get confused thinking that because we deserve to be punished for our sins, we are not worthy of love. Deserving and worthy are two different things. Most dictionaries miss the nuance between the two words. Therefore, I love Oxford dictionaries. To deserve is to: "Do something or have or show qualities worthy of (a reaction which rewards or punishes as appropriate)." Meanwhile, worthy is defined as: "sufficiently good, important, or interesting to be treated or regarded in the way specified." One is based on our actions. We get rewarded or punished based on what we have done. The other suggests inherent value or regard. That value or regard is based on one simple, yet profound fact. We are God's children, born of Him. Romans 8:16 says: "The Spirit himself testifies with our spirit that we are God's children" (NIV). We have an inherent value and worth in Him.

In retrospect, I wonder, why did I spend so much time trying to pay for my salvation? Salvation is not a reward for the good things we have done, so none of us can boast about it (See Ephesians 2:9). I worked hard, buried myself in church work, not purely out of gratitude for His gift, but rather with the mindset that I have to prove to God that I deserve it. There is a popular phrase I grew up hearing. In Jamaican parlance it is: "Nutten inna life nuh free. Yu eeda pay inna cash or wid kine." Translation: "Nothing in life is free. You pay for it one way or another."

I grew up in humble circumstances. Yes, there were many who helped along the way, but I had to watch my parents work very hard for everything we had. I was taught that nothing was handed to you on a platter and every opportunity or gift was a result of hard work. I missed the memo that it did not apply to salvation. It is free for me because Christ already paid the price.

We are worthy of love and worthy of His sacrificial death. Does it mean Christ deserved it? Not in the least. Crucifixion was not a just reward for what He brought to the table, for the miracles He performed or for the lives He changed. Yet, He gave Himself willingly because we are His and we are a love worth dying for. Christ offers the hope that we need so we don't have to do life alone. We are Christ's love and He saw us worthy of His ultimate sacrifice. Who are we to see ourselves as less? As you read this, I pray that you will verbally declare: "I am worthy of His Love. I am a love worth dying for." Now live like it.

Chapter Six

I Ran

Where shall I go from your Spirit? Or where shall I flee from your presence? (Psalm 139:7 – ESV).

I think everybody has a Bible character that just resonates with them, either consistently or during particular seasons. David, Gomer, and the Prodigal Son have been mine for different reasons and at different times. After Chris was killed, I became angry. It was not the kind of anger that often exploded. It was the kind that stewed and ate my heart, even when a smile was plastered on my face. It was the kind of anger that, even with my back straight and head held high, I was rotting inside. This anger brewed a form of spiritual apathy, wherein I was no longer interested in what my Father had to say. I was no longer interested in His direction, His opinion, or His will for my life. I had too many unanswered questions. I kept going to church or reaching out to people I believed were senior in the faith, hoping that somehow, they could tell me something that made sense. Instead, the chasm in my heart grew.

Worthy of Life and Love

To paint a picture of the scene of my heart, I can liken this time to a married couple who live in the same house but one partner has moved out of the intimacy of their marriage room to live in a guest room in the basement. That partner is so angry, that every word from the other strikes a chord of annoyance and disgust. Interaction is laboured and mechanical and only when necessary. In separate rooms, intimacy wains. I was the angry partner. God, in turn and only in retrospect, consistently, lovingly and patiently left reminders of His unending love. I was too mad to notice.

So, one day I point blank told Him I was done. "I'm going to do me. You can find me when You're able to answer my questions," was what I said. You know that book turned into a movie called "The Shack"? Recall that scene where Mack gets to the Shack and gets really mad and starts throwing stuff around and then spews the venom of his deepest emotion and weighed the thought of suicide. He threw the suicide thought out when he thought of how it would affect his family. Then, I am convinced that William P. Young had some sort of spy device in my mind when he penned these words because it was my exact thought: *"I'm done, God," he whispered. "I cannot do this anymore. I'm tired of trying to find You in all of this." And with that, he walked out the door. Mack determined that this was the last time he would go looking for God. If God wanted him, God would have to come find him* (William P. Young, The Shack). Mack was me and I was Mack.

In Luke 15, the Apostle tells the story of a son who had become impatient with his father's plan. In his frustration, he went to his father and, in not so subtle terms, told his father that he wanted his inheritance now. In other words, his father was dead to him so he should give him what he wanted. I cannot imagine the father's heartbreak. The father gives his son the inheritance and off the son goes living the dream, partying and such. Why did the father decide to give the son what he asked for? The father could have said no but he instead gave him the inheritance that he bargained for.

I am thinking that sometimes God will allow us to have what we want, to prove to us that it is not what we need. When all that we wanted loses its shine and the taste becomes bitter on our tongue, when we lose all that we want, we will find that what we needed, we had all along. I realised the father knew that in order to satisfy the questions in his son's heart, he had to let him go explore his desires to discover the deeper truth. Outside his father's house there is no peace. There is no joy. Outside his father's house, happiness and satisfaction are temporary. There is lack, suffering, pain, and hunger either physically, spiritually or both. Outside of a relationship with God, you can have things, maybe you can have your heart's desires, but you have no peace that passes understanding. Outside of a relationship with God, you will always miss out on the rivers of living water that quenches thirsts that we never knew we had. God, I have learned, remains constant and consistent in a world that is always changing. Mathematically speaking, in the equation of life, God is the unchanging given constant. Scientifically, even inert gases once thought to be completely unreactive, respond in extreme conditions but not God.

Running away for me did not appear overtly to the onlooker. I still went to church, occasionally. I did not change how I dressed, and I did not go out to parties. Instead, I drank more than my usual amounts of alcohol at home; I stopped reading the Word, and I definitely stopped praying and pursued comfort through relationships I would have otherwise shied away from. I do not recall saying to anyone that I was not a Christian anymore. Even though my facade appeared to be full of faith and standing firm, my heart was far from Him. For those close enough and bold enough to enquire, my answer was along the lines of: "God and I are in a strange place." I was the classic Isaiah 29:13 person: "And so the Lord says, "These people say they are mine. They honor me with their lips, but their hearts are far from me. And their worship of me is nothing but man-made rules learned by rote" (NLT). In other words, my outward appearance belied the position of my heart. My appearance and heart were not aligned.

So often we assume the prodigal sons and daughters are in the clubs at night or walking on the streets skimpily clad and hurling expletives. But if we could discern hearts, like God does, we would see that we sit beside prodigal children in church every Sunday. They walk around head held high, smile anchored brightly across their faces, an "amen" ready when needed and an "I'm blessed and highly favoured" retort for when someone casually attempts to check in. However, in their hearts they have no affinity or affection for God. It may not have started out that way and, for most, they do not consciously tell God: "I want nothing to do with You." Hurt, disappointment and frustration have built fortresses of stone around hearts once pliable to His will. They long to trust but they do not know how to. Their pain, invisible to those around them, proves in their minds, at least, that either God, or the people who are called by His name, must not be real. For myself, and for those who are in the position I was, God says: "I will give them an undivided heart and put a new spirit in them; I will remove from them their hearts of stone and give them a heart of flesh" (Ezekiel 11:19 – NIV). I cannot pinpoint when exactly this surgery began. I can only surmise the God of the impossible honoured His Word. As you read this, know that He will do the same for you.

The journey home for this prodigal daughter began when a friend who was running, like me, said something profound: "The best parts of you are the parts connected to God. Why are you running? Starting January, you are going to church. In fact, I'll come with you. End of conversation." I was not amused. I thought we were heading in the same direction, away from Father. Those words turned out to be like the fish that swallowed Jonah. I steamed over those words for days, annoyed at how God turned my escape plan into a detour back to His arms. When the words spat me back to shore I, I mean we, were heading in the direction of the Father's house. I was tired, broken, confused, with scarcely any energy to find my way back. My questions still unanswered, my intense fear, and all the reasons why taking me back as a daughter made no sense, were all burdens I shouldered on my journey. This time though, I committed to keeping my heart open to whatever He had to say. I was surprised by His response.

The story in Luke 15 tells us that the son rehearsed all that he had to say, expecting that he had to armour up to face his father. After all, he did, in a way, wish his father dead, walked away from his house and squandered his blessings. Have you ever felt terrified of approaching God? I used to get that morning-after feeling, that deep gut-wrenching feeling when I have failed. It is the weight of guilt that makes me feel unworthy of His Presence, much less His Love. These are times when I believe: "This is it Kavanaugh. God must be done with you now. There is no escaping fire and brimstone." Turns out God is not at all like I had imagined when I first believed. He is Love and His desire is that I do not perish in any area of my life.

Rehearsing his lines, the prodigal son starts the journey home. I imagine him repeating the lines over and over again. He must convince his father to give him a chance at working for penance. Instead, his father, seeing him in the distance heading in his direction and not even home yet, took his garment in hand and ran to his son. Pause a moment. The father saw him in the distance. I imagine he must have been looking out for him. In his heart, the father must have whispered: "Maybe today is the day my son will come home." Contrary to social norms where dignified men never lifted their coats or ran, the father, in his joy, did that for his son. The wayward son must have been as confused as I was when I discovered the truth that regardless of what I had done or where I had been or who I was, I am loved. I am worthy. I am His.

Placing a coat on his son's back, a ring on his finger, and sandals on his feet, the father threw the biggest party they had ever seen. So grand was this affair that the son who stayed home and remained faithful could hear the celebration from the field. When the father gave the wayward son lavish gifts, despite his betrayal, it was proof that his value as a son was not embedded in good works, getting it right or obligation. He was his son, full stop. We are sons and daughters because God adopted us with all the rights of a child. No amount of working to prove myself can repay God for all He does. Any works I can perform now, come from a position of being approved rather than one in which I am seeking approval. The difference may seem subtle but, for me, it was revolutionary. It means, I am not afraid of God in the sense of being terrified or anxious to approach God.

I am going to share something that you may laugh at, but I am being very serious. There was a time I was literally afraid that something ominous was pending for me. Cue lightning strike, freak accident, **something,** because I was convinced that God was angry with me and at any moment it would express itself in my sudden demise.

Like the prodigal son, my mental rhetoric, for a long time, had been "treat me like a hired servant." It is more comfortable to barter than to receive a luxurious gift with no probability of being able to pay it back. The prodigal son said: "I'm not worthy to be called son." The title "daughter" was a bit overwhelming and difficult to grasp. It is the reason I worked so hard. It is the reason I sometimes still struggle to believe that God wants to bless me and give me good things. This form of "slave psyche" opposes the truth of God's Word that reminds us that we are adopted into His family.

As I read the story again, I faced a new, hard truth. The way I see myself in relation to God affects how I pray. I remember one day recently, my son asked for something and before he waited for a response, he went on to say that he knows I will say no but he will ask anyway. It broke my heart. I told him that as my son it is his job to ask whatever he wants, and it is my job to assess whether it is good for him or not. I reminded him to ask, expecting that I will say yes but if I do say no, he should understand that mommy loves him so much that she will not give him something to harm him. The "no" is for his eventual benefit. I wish there was a narrator that would shout at that moment: "Ding ding ding. She got it folks!" Do you get it?

Chapter Seven

As A Man Thinks So Is He

For as he thinks in his heart, so is he. (Proverbs 23:7 - NKJV)

I am going to be as honest as I pride myself in being. Chronicling my story has been harder than I imagined it would be and as I wrote the title of this chapter, a sense of dread washed over my heart for a moment. Am I worth it? Am I good enough for the call of God on my life? Am I deserving of the privilege of the air I breathe? Can I truly say the title of this book "Worthy of Life and Love" without flinching?

I caught and continue to catch this negative self-talk and thought process and bring it into obedience to Christ. I am who He says I am. It is interesting that the Apostle Paul, with his sudden and miraculous conversion, did not document this moment as the process or method by which transformation comes. He said, "be transformed by renewing your mind" (See Romans 12:2). That verb "renewing" is in the present continuous format, which tells me it is a process. Change in my life comes when I change how I think. Old thought processes are like old wineskins. There is no way you can have new wine or newness in your life, if you keep pouring from old wineskins. "Kavanaugh, change your wineskin to change your life." In the past few years, God has been working on the wineskin of my perception of who He is.

I met Jesus in 1997, before my 15th birthday. I have been doing the church dance since. I have had so many significant experiences in church and have been trained in theology and doctrine. I have sat on committees and boards at churches; I have learned a lot of what I call "churchiology." I have had a tense but deep relationship with God, but I realised in the last few years that much of it was rooted in fear, works and religion. There was the fear of hell, fear that I was not doing something right or an assumption that in order to remain in God's good graces, I had to work hard to please Him. I thought I understood and appreciated His mercy and the grace He bestows on frail humanity. I subconsciously imagined a God who was angry with me all the time and He would feel sorry for me after my grovelling and let me get close again. I was so wrong. The genesis, the starting point, the essence of His mercy is buried and wrapped up in the fact that He is love. He does not only give love, feel love or show love, He **is** Love.

1st Corinthians 13 is really a description of the personhood of God. So, no I am not worthy of His Life or Love because I have done something to find favour in His eyes. I am worthy because He, being the embodiment, epitome, and essence of Love, willingly says I am. That Love is not keeping score of my wrongs or waiting for me to mess up so He can rejoice and zap me. No! Love is patient with us, with me. He knows my frame; He knows I am but dust. Yet, in this earthly vessel, He hides great treasure. He buries Himself. He did not give a messenger or an angel or some surrogate, He gave me Himself.

Have you ever been in a situation where someone was patiently trying to explain something to you, and you could not get it? Then, strangely, something just clicked, and the matter just became clear. That was me in church one Sunday morning after I moved to Canada. I was in a foreign place and no one knew who I was. The message was about Naomi, who had grown bitter because she lost her husband and she had to start over and find a new dream. You can understand that there are parallels with Naomi's story and mine. The message was: God loved Naomi deeply and even though she did not recognise it at that point, He had already prepared for her. I ugly cried for a long while during and after the service. It was as if I had an epiphany after the twenty years of Jesus telling me that He loves me. It just clicked. I am loved!

I remember, at some point in Sunday School, I learned this song: "Jesus love is very wonderful, it's so high that you can't get over it, it's so low that you can't get under it, it's so wide that you cannot get around it, oh wonderful love." Buried in the innocence of that childhood chorus is profound truth. God's love for you is complete and full. It cannot be earned, neither can you diminish it: you are loved, flaws and all. Understand that before you realised your need for Him, He was making a way for you to be with Him. Remember, while we were yet sinners, Christ died. It is liberating when you get this revelation. You do not have to pretend; you do not have to fight for God's love or attention. Sweetheart, you are the apple of His eye, chosen and royal. "Even before the world was made, God had already chosen us to be His through our union with Christ, so that we would be holy and without fault before Him. Because of His love, God had already decided that through Jesus Christ He would make us his children—this was His pleasure and purpose." (Ephesians 1:4-5 – GNT)

For the ladies who are hiding in the back, of which I use to be chief, God's love for you is full and complete. You cannot add to or subtract from it. That should cause you to walk a bit taller, smile wider and approach His throne bolder. I guarantee that something about the way you talk and the way you approach life will change in light of God's love for you. Grabbing this truth is the foundation on which self-worth and acceptance is based. Am I worthy? Are you? Well, since you are the apple of God's eye, with your name written on His palm, you were known before you were conceived, loved by Love, and Life gave His life so you could live, then yes you are worthy.

Worthy of what, Kavanaugh? I am glad you asked. You are worthy of the opportunities presented to you. Do not second guess yourself. There is no need to allow fear to paralyse you into inaction. Grab hold of that promotion, that job, that business idea. If you make a mistake or it does not work, then take the lessons learned from them but never question your worthiness. Failure is a life tool, a classroom, if you allow it to be. So, if you fail, keep getting up.

My sister, my brother, you are made by and for Love, both as a conduit and a receptacle. There is nothing in your past, present or future that prohibits you from experiencing Love in all His glorious facets. I walked around for a long time feeling as though I did not deserve the love I craved from friends, family or spouse. I have since learned that this is one of the ways the enemy keeps you from abundant living. He wants to steal your esteem, kill your faith, and destroy your life. How can you truly live with limitations on your heart? How can you truly accept a gift, if you feel unworthy of it? Let me prove an important point in His Word. God gave Moses the Ten Commandments as a standard of His expectations. From those Ten Commandments, scholars agree that 613 laws were written in the Old Testament. When Jesus entered the scene in the New Testament, the people recognized Him as an astute scholar of the Law. Even the Sadducees were unable to trap Him in matters of the Law (See Matthew 22). In Matthew 22:36, the Pharisees made their attempt to trap Him by asking the question, "What is the most important commandment in the Law?" Jesus' response made me pause. "Jesus replied, 'Love the Lord your God with all your heart and with all your soul. Love him with all your mind.' (Ref: Deuteronomy 6:5). This is the first and most important commandment. And the second is like it. 'Love your neighbour as you love yourself.' (Ref: Leviticus 19:18) Everything that is written in the Law and the Prophets is based on these two commandments." (Matthew 22:37-40 – NLT).

The 613 Old Testament laws are encapsulated into two commandments: Love God with your all and love your neighbour as you love yourself. We would all unanimously agree, without a second thought, that loving God is paramount. Loving others is a logical next step. However, the prerequisite for neighbourly love is self-love. You cannot truly love anyone else, without establishing love for yourself. This is necessary for you to maintain a healthy balance that does not endanger you and put you at risk of abuse. Love your neighbour as yourself is the golden rule for all earthly relationships, that is, do to others what you would have them do to you. Acts of hatred towards others are often born from a lack of self-love.

God's love in and through me should be my real motivation for all I do in God's Kingdom. It is not the other way around. It is actually prideful to believe that my work: all the serving, praying, piety I give, could ever measure up to the sacrifice of leaving Heaven's throne room to be clothed in frail flesh, then crucified for the sins He never committed. It is similar to an innocent person volunteering to take the death penalty, so that a confessed, known and guilty killer could live life freely. That is not a fair exchange and could never be. As grand and mind blowing as such a gesture would be, it pales in comparison to Jesus's gift. Yet, it has already been done. So, what should our response be? Accept it. It is a gift and it is paid for already, so take it. It is yours.

If you remember nothing else from this entire book, I need you to remember that you are loved completely and fully, without needing to add or subtract anything. Your journey through this earth requires growth and change, not to be loved but because you are loved by Love Himself. He thought you worthy of abundant life, so Life Himself died in your place. Now He is established at the right hand of God, making intercession for you and guaranteeing that regardless of the circumstance, as you see it now, the final outcome will accomplish incredible good.

Say it with me: "I am Worthy of Life and Love. I am enough and I lack nothing."

Section 2

"A Letter For You"

A Letter To My Younger Self

Dear Younger Me,

I know you hear it all the time: that you are beautiful and full of potential, but I know you do not believe it. You struggle with the conflict of self-doubt and the expectation from everyone else that you were meant to do great things. There is a divergence in your thought pattern. You instinctively realise that you are talented in many ways, but the fear of failure has you playing small. You know you are different, but you would give anything just to fit in. There is a duality in the worth you think you should own up to and the one you accept because your innocence was unwillingly stolen.

Unfortunately, this fear, this duality will hold you hostage for a long time, but it does not have to. The Bible says a double minded man is unstable in all his ways (See James 1:8). For you, it means you will take on many things and not truly focus on any one thing. It means you will accomplish many little things but inside you will ache knowing there is more you could do, had you zoned in and focused.

Younger Me, I know, practically, this letter will not find you, but I wanted to tell you something so crucial and so climatic to your journey. If you get this, no, *when* you get this revealed truth, you will absolutely not be the same. It is funny how simple it is. You have known (head knowledge) for a long time but you did not understand, so you did not walk in its wisdom. My dear, you are loved. You are loved by Love Himself. Life Himself put on flesh and walked this earth so you, my dear, would live abundantly. You are loved; you are worthy. This worth is not because there is anything you could work up to and not because all your efforts made Him decide that you are. You are loved simply because Love Himself knit you in your mother's womb, placed within you unique features, talents and fingerprints and then turned around and said to Himself, "Well done. What We have made is very good."

I know, I know they stole your innocence, poked holes in your confidence, and crippled your walk, all in an effort to have you not see Him. But God says: "I cried every time you did; I stored every tear and I have waged war for your life. Your only requirement is to accept My Gift, accept My Truth, and accept My Love. Trust Me and the hardest thing can be faced with a peace filled heart."

Dear Younger Me, despise not your humble beginnings; with God all things are possible.

For Your Journal:

If you could speak to your younger self, what would you say?

_____

_____

Kavanaugh Dickson Williams

Worthy of Life and Love

_____
_____
_____
_____
_____
_____
_____

Get into your quiet space and listen for God's voice gently whispering to your soul. Write down what you hear.

_____
_____
_____
_____
_____
_____
_____
_____

Now research the words you heard in Scripture (Google is your friend). Write down the Scripture that matches what you heard.

_____
_____
_____

Kavanaugh Dickson Williams

A Letter To The Widow

Dear Widow,

I remember on the day of Christopher's funeral, as they lowered his casket in the ground, the finality of the moment hit hard. He was home for me. He was my future. The blueprint for my tomorrows and my best-laid plans were being buried too. He was the priest of our home and our leader. In that moment, I noted that his voice would never calm the tumult of my emotions again or give wisdom where there was doubt. So, I stood there for several minutes just staring, wondering what would be next. Yes, I thought maybe ending my life and joining him would make more sense with such certainty that I bought two burial plots.

It is dark right now and navigating beyond the next moment seems implausible. It is. You cannot fathom, imagine or comprehend life beyond right now and that is perfectly normal, but it is not impossible. Some months ago, a conversation about the day of the funeral came up with a friend of mine. She said that in the moment I stood staring into the distance, rendered motionless by grief and anxiety of not knowing my next move, a crowd of supporters standing quietly and motionless behind me. I was not aware of their presence. In fact, it may have felt awkward or overwhelming.

But they stood there bearing me up in love and prayer without me knowing, until I was ready to take the next step to the car.

I imagine this scene was a physical representation of a spiritual truth. The prophet Elisha prayed that his servant would have his eyes opened so he could see that there were more for him than they that were against him (See 2 Kings 6). You will feel lonely but remind yourself that you are not actually alone. Healing is a process guided by choice. You can let the pain dictate your course and choose to remain emotionally dead. You can choose to shut down your heart and let the fear of losing someone else you love prevent you from giving of yourself. Hardened hearts build walls that shut out all types of deep, emotional connections, sometimes unintentionally.

In my devotional, I spoke about grief not being something you get over like a bridge you cross to get to the other side that is filled with joy and peace. Rather, it is a new normal. In your new normal you can hold on so tightly to pain that you experience nothing else. Here is the good news. You can choose to heal, to love and to grow from this. Today, my grief waves are not less potent or frequent but my ability to process and recover from each onslaught is better.

Dear Widow, let the light in. I know even the title carries an indescribable burden. It is a scarlet letter of sorts. It is a brand of shame and pity to have met this fate and insecurities abound. I will not provide any bland clichés or tasteless band-aids to disguise your wound. As you redesign your life that is made for two to fit an equation equal to one, I will say this: with the same Spirit that rose Christ from the dead and having trod this road but a few moments ago, I declare you are worthy of the air you breathe. You will live to declare God's goodness in the land of the living and every wall you have built to shut the light out will crumble. There is purpose and passion in you yet undiscovered and you will find it. You will hone it and you will walk in freedom. This freedom will permit you to laugh so hard your stomach will hurt and cry until it does not. I declare strength to your soul and a determination to live fully. In this club, we are too familiar with the concept that life is short. Embrace that and live like it.

For Your Journal:

If money were not an issue, list ten things you would love to do.

_____
_____
_____
_____
_____
_____
_____
_____
_____
_____

Worthy of Life and Love

_____
_____
_____
_____
_____

Create a vision board with your top five things. I want you to have a visual of what you can do with your life and make a plan to head towards it.

A Letter To The Married Singles

Dear Married Single Woman,

I know there are a few who may not understand the phrase "Married Single Woman" but this is for those who do. It is a lonely space to be in a committed relationship such as marriage but the circumstances of your life dictate a single person existence. This is for the woman whose husband lives/works in another country/area and you are in each others' physical presence a few times a month or year. Or the woman whose marriage is so broken that, while married, you have to operate as though you lived alone or as though you have no one else to lean on and "do life" with. You, my sis, are married single.

I remember the frustration I felt one weekend around the last Christmas at church prior to writing this book. There was an event for married folks. Couples were invited to fellowship with other married people. I did not want to go there alone. My husband lives thousands of miles away. Then there was the fellowship and support event for the single parents. Well then, to claim to be single while being in a committed marriage relationship did not sit well with me. I felt single in the sense that the full weight of raising the boys in my day to day was on me. The struggle to pick up and drop off at school, finding a caregiver, if I needed to go somewhere, or the panic of being late for pick up because no one else is nearby who can do it; the packing of lunches and the homework coaching are all responsibilities that fell on me. When I get home from a long day at work, there is no one there to physically comfort me. I did not fit into either category because I am married single.

I am going to be honest. For a while, I lived deeply frustrated and miserable. It took me a while to wrap my head and heart around this state of being. I did not get married to live "single." In a world where everything is labelled and packaged, it feels strange to not quite fit. It is a struggle knowing that you are legally and spiritually allowed to have your sexual needs met but not be able to. For the married singles separated by distance, keeping the lines of communication is our biggest challenge. For those in the same physical space, keeping your heart free from anger and bitterness feels like a full-time job. As the world bombards you with options to bend or break your commitment, it takes strength to remain faithful to your vows.

My sister, if you are experiencing the married single life in this season, I want to encourage you. It is a difficult winter but spring has to come. "As long as the earth remains, there will be planting and harvest, cold and heat, summer and winter, day and night" (Genesis 8:22 - NLT). In other words, it is God's design that the earth, and all that is in it, operates in seasons. No season is permanent but each one serves a purpose. Winter is underrated and sometimes hated but it is crucial to the planet's survival. Your personal winters are important for your growth. I know it sucks. I am not even trying to sugar-coat it. But hear me well: we have all we need to thrive already within us. Remember your first Love, Your *Ishi* (the Lord your Husband). His love is complete and constant. I have felt Him calm my tantrums and subside my raging hormones because I was honest and vulnerable with my heart before Him.

Do not (as I did for some time) allow yourself to feel like your life is on pause, waiting for this season to change or things to be fixed. It made me utterly miserable. The truth is, there will never be a time when every aspect of your life is perfect. Our job, therefore, is to be grateful for all of it. The curveballs in my life, though painful, taught me more about my awesome, loving eternal Father than theology, doctrine or peaceful times ever did. Look for the lessons, hold on to moments of joy, and laugh for heaven's sake. Change is coming.

For Your Journal:

Think of a season (before this one) that was really difficult. How did it conclude and what lessons did you learn then that helps you with now?

Worthy of Life and Love

A Letter To The Single Parent

Dear Superhuman,

Yes you. I am convinced that single parents are given an extra something from God to take care of His precious ones. I remember about a month before Christopher died, I lay exhausted on the couch from a long day and he took over the care of the boys. The thoughts came, "Single parenting is not the original design; how do single parents do this?" Parenting is hard with two, even with the help of my mom and a twice a week housekeeper. I grew this overwhelming and odd (because it felt so random) respect for people who raise children alone. Little did I know it was soon to be my own plight.

I do not know how you got here. For most, it was not the plan but then life hits you like a freight train and you have two choices: give up or put the "S" on your chest and make do with the resources you have. I know there are days you wish there was an exit door you could slip through, but your children need you and you know it. I was intentional about the word "resource" because, truth is, you cannot do it alone.

The "S" on your chest does not just mean super, it is for "sourcer". You are responsible for sourcing the help your children need to be healthy. That help may be basic physical needs, emotional or spiritual ones. Swallow your pride and ask for the help you need. The Scripture says you have not because you ask not (See James 4:2). Sometimes resources and programs are underutilized because people do not ask or apply. Let it not be that your child lacks because you did not ask.

Superhuman, do not buy into the lie that you absorb the role of the other parent. Ladies, you can never be a father. You cannot teach your sons the intricacies of manhood or show your daughter how men should treat women. Gents, you can never be a mother. You cannot teach your daughter the subtleties of womanhood or provide the softer side of nurturing needed to balance the natural roughness of men. However, you can source healthy connections who are trustworthy to play the role, all while remaining vigilant on what they are feeding into your children's psyche and spirit. Immerse yourself in community; it really does take a village to raise a child.

Finally, Superhuman, REST. Even Jesus, Creator of the universe, took time away from the crowds and all that His ministry demanded of Him to rest, pray and hear what the Father required of Him. God says He gives His beloved rest (See Psalm 127:2). You are His beloved. Figure out a way to take time for yourself every day. Exercise and engage in a hobby: something that is absolutely for you and nothing to do with the kids and the hundreds of other things you often put above your own self-care. The moment you stop pouring into yourself, you start shortchanging your children, career and pretty much everything in your life. Your children need you to be the best version of yourself so they can learn to do the same.

For Your Journal:

Make a list of the things you enjoy doing alone.

_____
_____
_____
_____
_____
_____
_____
_____

Think of some simple self-care activities that interest you that you can do at home when the children are sleeping or involved in an activity. For example, facials, manicures, a long bath instead of a shower, experimenting with makeup, etc.

_____
_____
_____
_____
_____
_____
_____

Now set aside some time at least once per week to incorporate one or more of these activities.

A Letter To The Woman Seeking Love

Dear Love Seeker,

At the risk of oversimplification, I am putting three categories out there. There are those who are happy to be single, those who are guarded single and those who are so anxious for Adam's arrival, that his absence washes you with dread that he has a broken GPS. So, I will start with the happily single.

You, my dear, are in absolutely no rush to get hitched. Anybody coming your way must be so close to perfect that he could be snatched up like Enoch at a moment's notice. If you did not catch that analogy, refer to Genesis 5. You are happy in your own skin and you enjoy your own company. You are a whole person on your own and you do not subscribe to the fallacy that you need a mate to complete you. You would be content if you never got married. Kudos to you because many women struggle with the concept of singleness. Since you are technically not seeking love, this letter is not for you.

On the surface, guarded singles have all the trimmings of the happily single, but your heart position is different. You want love and marriage and may sense that God is directing you towards that path, but you are terrified to let your guard down. Pain has caused you to erect a fortress around your heart and you would rather push relationships away, than come face to face with human intimacy. I have some advice for you.

Let me begin with the neon colored "Unavailable: I do not want or need a man" sign on your forehead. Men can spot it right away. If you are not sure you are wearing one, here are a few hints, though all may not apply. You are carrying something heavy, maybe not beyond your ability to carry but definitely beyond comfort level and a gentleman offers his help, and you refuse it. How about that blank or stone face you automatically put up as a defence the moment the opposite sex speaks to you? Not every man speaking to you has a motive beyond conversation or friendship. Finally, let us pull back on the rhetoric that ALL men are ____. You can fill in the blank with all your broad sweeping generalisations born out of your pain, past or your need to preserve your purity.

Marriage is beautiful when there is mutual submission. I worry for my guarded single friends who are so fiercely independent that they refuse to yield. You are so used to not needing a partner that the concept of mutual submission irritates you. It is present in attitudes like insisting on your way of doing things all the time or resisting a suitor's well-intentioned advice without truly weighing its merit. Now if you are called to remain single for life, this is a non-issue. However, if marriage is a part of God's plan for you, then you will need to learn the strength in surrender. You will need to be flexible in planning your days and you must trust that God has your best interest at heart. Men love to chase but hate to feel like they are wasting their time. Godly men know that Eve is meant to be a helpmate, not a burden, so he will value what you bring to the table but remain humble. So, during the chase, leave clues to let him know what he is doing well and tell him when he is off-track. Men ultimately need to feel useful, so invite his help into your tasks. We can compare this to an escalator. You technically do not need them to climb stairs, but it is helpful if there is one to get you to the next level. If this is God's call on your life, prepare to level up.

To my sisters waiting impatiently for Adam to win the game of hide and seek by finding you tucked neatly away in an inconspicuous corner, I say relax. He is coming, if it is God's will for you. In the meantime, enjoy the season you are in. Fully immerse yourself in what God has called you to and if you are not sure what that is, get planted in a Bible-believing church, submit to leadership there and volunteer your time. "Bae" is not going to find you when you are at home watching Netflix and hiding behind one screen or another. Prepare yourself to be the best version of you so that when you receive God's gift, you will not ruin it. Trust me, my unhealed places almost cost me my first marriage and we had to fight very hard to get to a better place. I do not want that for you. When you go into companionship whole, you will spend more time enjoying the adventure that is marriage rather than battling for your emotional and spiritual health. This is not to

Worthy of Life and Love

say that all sisters waiting for Adam are somehow not well or this is the cause for your singleness. What I am saying is that if there are areas that you can work on, do it during the wait.

For Your Journal:

What are the areas in your heart that you think need healing? Don't just skim over this; pray about it and be vulnerable enough before God for Him to point out the thing He wants to work on now.

_____
_____
_____
_____
_____
_____
_____
_____
_____
_____
_____
_____
_____
_____
_____

A Letter To The Divorcee

Dear Divorcee,

This is perhaps the only marital status I have not worn, so forgive me for not being able to be deeply personal with this one. I will say though that divorce reminds me of grieving when a relationship ends. That I know about. Your divorce certificate, your memories documented and undocumented, children, if you have any, are the tangible bits of proof that you (plural) existed. No one goes into marriage thinking it is a short-term plan. Even if there is turmoil in your relationship, you somehow hope that the firmness of the commitment will improve things.

I know the pain of that math. One plus one should have become two, but it became one instead. Now you must be two again. How is that possible when fragments of your soul are now his? Now you must un-share friends, finances, habits, experiences and a path designed for two must be walked alone. Looking at your life, it is like scuff marks on a beautiful painting. It is hard to look at, without seeing the blemishes and cringing. Pain is universal and, while I cannot identify with your specific brand, I know well the pain of losing a relationship that once meant everything. It hurts. Deeply. Sometimes inexpressibly.

Here is the thing: I pray that by the time you get to this page, your worthiness is already blatantly obvious. Daughter of the living God, your Maker is your Husband and He knows how to treat you right. His promise has always been to never leave you and He never has. Even when you are faithless, God remains faithful because He cannot deny Himself (See 2 Timothy 2:13). He's got you, lady!

For Your Journal:

Now you have some homework. Acknowledge the part you played in your relationship failing. Even if you believe he messed up more than you did, you are awesome, not perfect, so get that pen and write it down. You cannot forgive what you have not acknowledged. I mean it, put the book down and get to writing.

_____
_____
_____
_____
_____
_____
_____
_____
_____
_____
_____

_____

_____

_____

When you are done, ask God to forgive you. He is faithful and just to do that. Here is the hard part: forgive yourself. By that I mean release yourself from mulling over the mistakes repeatedly. Do not let them define you. Do not claim them as character flaws or "that's just who I am." Commit instead to learn from them.

What are my triggers? What led me to react that way? In project management, we have a document done at the end of a project or phase called a "lessons learned" document. I want you to take the time to document your lessons learned.

> "Those who cannot remember the past are condemned to repeat it." ~ George Santayana.

What are the things you have learned about yourself and about what you want in a relationship? Keep this as a working file that you will keep adding to.

_____

_____

_____

_____

_____

_____

Worthy of Life and Love

Finally, I want you to destroy the list you wrote with the mistakes. Jesus cast our sins and mistakes into the sea of forgetfulness, so you don't need to go diving in to retrieve it. When you mess up, learn the lesson, forgive yourself and move on. Give yourself permission to live and love again: this time, with the wisdom of all the lessons you learned and the knowledge that you are worth it.

A Letter To The Married Woman

Dear Mrs. You,

Your heart often swells with gratitude and pride when you think of God's gift to you in terms of marriage. Sometimes you catch yourself wondering what could ever break you, but you shove the thought aside and focus on the good; as you should. There are many resources out there with tips on how to be a better partner or to maintain and strengthen your marriage, so this letter will not go there. In fact, I will be brief.

Remain grateful for your gift. Marriage, or any deep, meaningful relationship, has highs and lows, ebbs and flows. Sometimes it is easier to look at all that is going wrong and lose track of the reasons you started in the first place. I beg you, remain grateful. It is a pretty simple command; "in everything give thanks; for this is the will of God in Christ Jesus for you" (1 Thessalonians 5:18 - NKJV). Did you know that the concept of thankfulness shows up 102 times in the Old Testament and 71 times in the New Testament? Gratitude is a pretty big deal.

There were times in the first years of my marriage to Chris that I had forgotten to be grateful for all he was. Difficult times, counselling and practicing gratitude fixed that over time. It is a lesson I took into my second marriage. I am absolutely grateful for my husband. I am grateful for who he is, who he is not and for the ways we add to each others' lives. When I focus on those things, the trivialities shrink, and my husband is even more wonderful in my eyes. Pay attention to the toothpaste on the counter or the toilet seat up or the way he chews his food long enough, and those trivialities will become like water slowly dripping at night or a mosquito you cannot quite see buzzing in your ear. Everything else will slowly spiral out of balance and you will not have brain or heart space to allow the good that he is to be at the forefront. Seriously, who can focus on anything with that annoying mosquito sound in your ear?

Listen, I am not saying be grateful for abuse or that you should stay in an abusive, life threatening (emotional, spiritual or physical) situation. Yes, I have learned to be grateful for the lessons taught in retrospect but I would not wish abuse for even my enemy. We need to distinguish between preferences and principles. Is this thing that you are huffy about a principle or a preference? A principle determines the direction your life is going in; it underpins your goals, morals; your *raison d'etre*. A preference is something like: "I like the color gold and he likes black" or "I like the toilet seat down; he prefers it up." Adjust to each others' preference. It is a trade-off; give and take. Principles are a whole other story.

I remember the day before Chris died. We were driving home and we got into a conversation about gratitude. In that conversation, he laid out all the things he observed in me recently that was making him grateful to God for me and I did the same. We were at a good place. We both openly expressed that we were grateful and why. You know what that did for me after he passed? I was free of the guilt of unsaid things. I had no regrets that he did not know how I felt or why, and I do not live wondering if, in the end, our marriage was healed of all the stuff that went wrong in the beginning. That freedom makes me unafraid to give or receive love and it makes me even more adamant that gratitude in everything is God's will for me. When I start panicking about my situations, I know for certain that I have lost sight of gratitude. So, I dial back on the worry and make a mental list of the things I have to be grateful for.

So, Mrs. You, with this letter, my encouragement is simple: remain grateful for your gift.

For Your Journal:

Make that list of things about the Mr. that you are grateful for (nothing is too big or small). Do not overthink it, just write:

_____
_____
_____
_____
_____

Worthy of Life and Love

_____
_____
_____
_____
_____
_____
_____

Make an event of it (be creative) and share your list with him.

Now That I Know

Writing this book has been an emotional and vulnerable process. It took me as long as it did to write because during each chapter, the encouragement I shared was challenged in my own heart. God applied balm to my heart and did deeper surgery. Maybe reading it has exposed a shard of glass pushing its way to the surface. You may be thinking: I get that I am loved; that I am worthy but what do I do next? What does worthy look like in my day to day life? I wish this is where I could give you a seven-step guide to walking worthy. The truth is, your next step is totally dependent on where you are on your journey and what God needs to deal with now.

In my vision, at the end of this, I would share with you some physical evidence that said: Look, I have got my life together now and everything is perfect. I cannot. Not truthfully. Currently, I am employed in a role a few notches below my qualifications, I am married-single and trying to adjust to life in Canada with two amazing, energetic and demanding boys. Also, I am deeply home sick. Yet, I have come to understand a far deeper truth: It is well with my soul. There is pain but a steadiness that says: I really do not understand this desert, this waiting period but I know the God I serve loves me deeply. I know that if He is allowing this season, there is a purpose in it. I know it is not what we want to hear. We still imagine that Him loving us means He swoops in on a white horse and saves the day from all turmoil every time. We imagine that God's blessing is only present in physical things. But the God who makes summer also made winter to accomplish a deeper purpose in the earth. In the same way, our wintery, dry, desert, wilderness, whatever we may call it season, is meant to accomplish deeper things in our hearts.

My last bit of advice is this: allow yourself to be vulnerable before God. He lovingly awaits your presence at His feet exactly as you are. He will not ask you to fix yourself. There may be some things that resonate with you throughout the book; focus on the gentle promptings and ask God what He needs you to do next. Do not close your mind to the possibility of professional therapy, getting a trustworthy mentor or accountability partner or forgiving your abuser. I encourage you to write what is on your heart in a journal; physical or digital. Let the truth that you are worthy find itself on good soil, and then water it with the Word. Find Scripture related to the things that affect you and declare them over your life, not from a place of ritualism or religion, but from the perspective that the pages of Scripture are His love letter to you. Remind yourself of what He thinks of you.

Section 3 includes affirmations that you can declare over your life, until they find root in your soul. Add to them as the King of your heart whispers His healing Word to you.

My sister, I remind you that you are loved.

"For this reason, since the day we heard it, we have not ceased praying for you and asking that you may be filled with the knowledge of God's will in all spiritual wisdom and understanding, so that you may lead lives worthy of the Lord, fully pleasing to him, as you bear fruit in every good work and as you grow in the knowledge of God. May you be made strong with all the strength that comes from his glorious power, and may you be prepared to endure everything with patience, while joyfully giving thanks to the Father, who has enabled you to share in the inheritance of the saints in the light. He has rescued us from the power of darkness and transferred us into the kingdom of his beloved Son." (Colossians 1:9-13 – NRSV).

Section 3

"Affirmations"

Daily Affirmations

The Scripture encourages us in Romans 12:2: "And do not be conformed to this world, but be transformed by the renewing of your mind, that you may prove what is that good and acceptable and perfect will of God" (NKJV).

I have included 21 Scripture-based affirmations in this next section to help capture the negative thoughts that go against what God has declared in His Word about us. If you are reading a print copy of this book, feel free to cut these out and walk with them or place them where they are visible.

Day 1

I am made in the image of God and in His likeness. I was made to have dominion over the things that concern me in the earth. (See Genesis 1:26).

Day 2

I have more than enough because He is my Shepherd and I lack nothing. (See Psalm 23:1).

Day 3

I am fearfully and wonderfully made. I have no reason to dwell in a place of insecurity about my body, worth or purpose. (See Psalm 139: 14).

Day 4

I am the apple of God's eye. My name is inscribed in His palms and I was known long before I was conceived. My birth was intentional, and I am filled with potential. (See Psalm 17:8, Isaiah 49:16, Psalm 139:13).

Day 5

No greater love hath a man than this, that he should lay down his life for a friend. God is my friend and He gave up His life for me so I will make my life count. I am worthy of Life. (See John 15:13).

Day 6

GOD is within me; I will not fail. (See Psalm 46:5).

Day 7

I am Worthy of Love because God, who is Love, decided to make me His child through Christ. (See Ephesians 1:5). It is His pleasure and purpose for me. (See Philippians 2:13).

Day 8

God has a purpose and a good plan for my life that I can only discover through Him. So, I will seek Him and find Him. (See Jeremiah 29:13).

Day 9

I will ask and receive an answer about my future because my God, who created all things, says I should ask. (See Jeremiah 33:2).

Day 10

I will remain confident in God's love, regardless of the circumstances I see with my eyes. His love is faithful. (See Isaiah 54:10).

Day 11

My life will silence every voice that raises up to accuse me because that is my benefit as God's child. None of the weapons formed against me will be successful in the end. (See Isaiah 54:17).

Day 12

I am clothed with strength and dignity, and I laugh without fear of the future. (See Proverbs 31:25).

Day 13

I will not forget God's goodness towards me. My life is filled with good things. (See Psalms 103:5).

Day 14

God's love for me is unfailing and infinite. I cannot earn it. I cannot do anything to make Him love me more or love me less. (See Psalm 103:11 & 17).

Day 15

I am chosen, royal and holy. I will proclaim God's awesomeness for He has called me out of darkness into light. (See 1 Peter 2:9).

Day 16

I am neither fearful nor weak. God's Spirit in me is powerful. God's Spirit in me is love that conquers all. God's Spirit in me creates discipline. (See 2 Timothy 1:7).

Day 17

I can do all things through Christ who gives me strength. (See Philippians 4:13).

Day 18

I will not act in fear or retreat because I am dismayed. God is with me; He will help me, He will strengthen me, He will uphold me. (See Isaiah 41:10).

Day 19

I am worthy of Life. "I have been crucified with Christ. It is no longer I who live, but Christ who lives in me. And the life I now live in the flesh I live by faith in the Son of God, who loved me and gave himself for me." (Galatians 2:19b-20 – NKJV).

Day 20

Nothing can separate me from God's love. Absolutely nothing. (See Romans 8:38–39).

Day 21

God loved me when I did not even recognize or acknowledge His existence and made a plan to introduce Himself. I am loved. (See Romans 5:8).

About The Author

Kavanaugh Dickson Williams is a Best-Selling Author, Speaker and blogger for "Lady Kavan Writes." Her first devotional "Grief Stricken" was written after the tragic loss of her first husband. She has experienced many seasons of loss and triumphs but now believes that God's grace and love has been the only constant in her life. Her writing is intended to help others navigate complex emotions in the context of the Bible.

She began her journey of faith more than twenty years ago, while living in St. Catherine, Jamaica. She now attends Brampton Christian Family Church in Ontario Canada, where she participates in children's ministry as a teacher. She is wife to Carlton, and mother to Matthew and Isaiah. Professionally, she is a certified Project Manager with a MBA from the University of New Orleans. She has a certificate in Biblical Foundation from Whole Life College in Kingston, Jamaica.

www.ingramcontent.com/pod-product-compliance
Lightning Source LLC
Chambersburg PA
CBHW071310060426
42444CB00034B/1760